TEACHING ENGLISH ABROAD
All Things TEFL for Native and Non-native English Teachers

BY
ANDREW WILLIAM

TEFL LESSON PLANS
Samples, Strategies, Tools and Activities
is now on promotion at Amazon.com

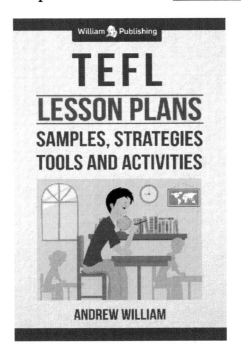

TEFL Lesson Plans is a ready-made course manual for both current and new ESL teachers. The book is full of useful tops and strategies that will aid you in creating fun and engaging lesson plans to deliver effectively to your students.

TABLE OF CONTENTS

Preface

One day a man who had been out to gather coconuts loaded his horse heavily with the fruit. On the way home he met a boy whom he asked how long it would take to reach the house.

"If you go slowly," said the boy, looking at the load on the horse, "you will arrive very soon; but if you go fast, it will take you all day."

The man could not believe this strange speech, so he hurried his horse. But the coconuts fell off and he had to stop to pick them up. Then he hurried his horse all the more to make up for lost time, but the coconuts fell off again. Many times he did this, and it was night when he reached home.

Source: Mabel Cook Cole, Philippine Folk Tales
(Chicago: A. C. McClurg, 1916), p. 88

The man's intention all along was to get the fruit home; he just hadn't yet perfected his technique on how exactly to go about doing so. This can be equated to teaching, as there is no set method to follow. But becoming a good teacher and learning how to get the best out of your students is something that comes with gradual practice; it's not something that needs to be rushed in order to get best results.

This book has been designed for both current and future English as a Second Language (ESL) teachers, by an experienced English teacher; who has taught in a variety of countries across the globe, in both public schools and private institutions, and to a wide range of different students.

It provides you with a complete step-by-step guide on how exactly to land yourself with the best possible teaching position, and why you should even consider teaching ESL abroad in the first place. It discusses what it's actually like to live in a different country as an expat, and advises you on the best ways to fully embrace and immerse yourself in a new culture.

It's also jam-packed with useful tips and strategies for the challenges that one encounters in the classroom, and everything else that tends to surface at a foreign school on a daily basis. The book is also furnished throughout with highly regarded and well-researched information to give you proven methods of implementation to equip you on the road to becoming a successful teacher; and on really getting the most out of your journey.

It gives realistic accounts on what it's like to teach in a foreign school environment; and doesn't promote the idyllic "Leave your nine-to-five desk job and live happily ever after" picture that is so often painted when it comes to teaching English as a foreign language. Although, having said that, the thoughts of freezing-cold winter tube-rides to work in rainy London are a very distant memory, especially after experiencing the delights of: Vietnamese mountain backdrops; crystal-clear waters of the Philippines; the neon-lit cities of South Korea; and the historic, cherry blossomed and cobbled streets of Japan.

Having the opportunity to move around and live and teach in different countries across the world is truly a fantastic experience; although, at times it's a roller coaster ride filled with ups and downs. This book will help you to avoid some of the pitfalls that so often arise as you go on this journey of self-growth. It will hopefully bring to fruition the pleasure of the giving something back to people too: whether it be by seeing the joy and sheer gratitude on the face of an eleven-year old Thai boy as he fist-pumps the air after passing his English exam; or the self-satisfaction of watching your students grow and utilise what you have taught them in real-life conversations.

PART I - Prepare to Teach Abroad

Chapter One: Why Should You Teach English Abroad?

Travel the World and Save Money

There is a whole world out there just waiting for you to explore. Sustaining travel can be expensive however; and if you don't budget your finances correctly, lack of funds can leave you sleeping rough for a week or two down by a riverside – believe me, I know. Luckily for you, by financing travel with a well-paying Teaching English as a Foreign Language (TEFL) job, you can visit the most exotic places on Earth.

Venture to countries in Asia or the Middle East, and you could save over 50% (or even up to 80% depending how frugal you want to be) of your salary, and receive additional benefits like free airfare and housing. You'll also be perfectly situated location-wise in order to take full advantage of the cheap airfares that allow you make short hops to nearby countries. Teaching English is truly an amazing way to save money for travelling and/or combating those pesky student loan re-payments.

There is a Huge Job Market

With close to a billion budding English language learners worldwide, it naturally follows that there is a high demand for English teachers. Whether you're a recent university graduate or merely looking for a change of career, the job market for teaching English abroad is so vast that virtually anyone can make the transition.

You don't always need to hold a degree or have any prior teaching experience, but you should seriously consider taking an accredited TEFL certification course.

Make a Difference to the Kids

Even if you can't always fluently communicate with your students, it's often evident in their mannerisms and faces that you have inspired them in some way. Learning English can dramatically pave the way for their success whether it is academically, professionally or socially.

Sharing knowledge and experiences with the children will give you a great sense of accomplishment, and pride in your work.

Meet New People From All Over the World

Are you tired of always meeting the same types of people from your hometown or current circle of friends? If so, then branch out and teach English abroad - where you'll be frequently meeting people who speak different languages to you, as well as mingling with the locals from your chosen destination, and just generally encountering people from all walks of life.

In addition to this, you are guaranteed to meet plenty of like-minded fellow expats. These are the people you will make long-lasting friendships with. People who have the courage to teach abroad are typically adventurous, smart and social - so you will have plenty of like-minded people to hang out with.

Learn the Ways of the Local Culture

A two-week holiday in Spain or Mexico can be fun don't get me wrong, but it doesn't quite offer the same experience and thrills that you will encounter by immersing yourself in the daily life and culture of a foreign country.

You will - without any shadow of a doubt - surprise yourself at the exciting situations and surroundings that you find yourself in. And maybe even more remarkably, be impressed at the situations you'll manage to get yourself out of - whether it be riding to work on a tuk-tuk or a clapped-out moped, haggling at local street-markets, dining with locals (and communicating with hand gestures), or exploring mystical temples. It's also very likely that you'll be invited by your local friends and co-workers to weddings, celebrations, and/or traditional gatherings - all in all it will give you opportunities that a short holiday never could.

Personal Growth

Packing up your entire life into a suitcase and moving abroad to teach might seem daunting at first, but it will be the best decision you will ever make. You will become more independent, gain more life experience than you could have ever imagined, and make incredible memories that last a lifetime.

There's no denying it, living overseas does change you for the better, and even after just a couple of months you'll begin to look at yourself in a different light. It really does give you a fantastic opportunity to learn and stand on your own two feet by making you push yourself to approach strangers, by facing challenging new activities, by trying new food, by cleaning your own apartment, by adjusting to language barriers, by inspiring eager young minds and by working with people from all over the world.

Rediscover Your Fitness and Try New Hobbies

Work hours tend to be between 25 to 30 hours a week without compromising a full salary - so you can enjoy a more relaxed and healthier lifestyle.

As you will have more time on your hands without those lengthy commutes in the western rat-race, why not cleanse the soul and try out some new activities? You could do Yoga in India, Kung Fu in China, Meditate in Japan, Taekwando in South Korea, or try out some Muay Thai in Thailand.

Learn a New Language

In my opinion, immersion is a more effective way to learn a language compared with taking a foreign language course. Teaching abroad gives you an invaluable opportunity to learn a new language from your local friends, colleagues and even your students.

You will be teaching in a country where English is not the first language - so take advantage of that. Chances will arise daily for you to expose yourself to the new language, and you will soon find yourself picking-up and speaking local lingo. It also shows that you are respectful to the country that you have chosen to live in, and the locals will always be impressed at your efforts. Don't forget, you can also add your newly acquired language skills to your resume as well.

Gain a New Skill Set

We've all worked those unfulfilling shifts as a bartender, or as an office monkey - and wondered if this is really what we want to be doing. Teaching abroad does give you a fantastic route away from this; and enables you to wave goodbye to that menial path, and make a difference to the world (even if it is a small one).

Teaching gives you an arsenal of skills you can use in the future and it also transfers very well to other trades. It supplies you with expertise on how to manage a group of people, you'll learn education theory, become a master of the English language, and learn leadership and time-management skills. Most importantly, it will also provide you with precious interpersonal skills which you will learn from constantly dealing with people in different scenarios.

Boost Your Resume

Teaching ESL abroad will serve you well in the highly competitive economy of the twenty-first century. Employers in the current global climate seek people who have international work experience.

Taking on a job in a foreign country will set you apart from other candidates as it demonstrates your willingness to move out of your comfort zone, and it shows your ability to tackle challenges and adapt to a new environment.

Chapter Two: What to Expect From Teaching English Abroad

One of the common misconceptions about teaching in a foreign land is that it's an occasion to have a year of freedom and travel. But don't forget that it's ultimately a job, and not a holiday; you're a teacher, and not a backpacker.

That's not to say that teaching ESL abroad doesn't provide ample opportunities to travel and have fun; in fact the excitement of living in a new region is one of the biggest lures for people. Just be prepared to work professionally and remember that honouring the commitments that you have made to your employer and students is of profound importance.

Exploring what it's like to actually be a teacher and setting yourself some realistic expectations as to what will be required to teach overseas will help you get the most out of your adventure.

If You're Dreaming of Travel - Then Just Travel

Teaching ESL generally gets advertised as a way to fund your travels; however, you won't be fully escaping the delights of the nine-to-five lifestyle back home. When you teach ESL abroad, you will have to do all the things that people have to do when they have a real job - because it is a real job.

If your reasoning behind choosing to teach abroad is purely to travel, then you should just travel, or consider taking a gap year as the job in hand may become like an unwanted chore. Like most real jobs out in the world, teaching English is a lot of hard work. You have to be prepared to put some genuine effort into the job, or you're going to end up feeling unhappy; and also, doing a great disservice to your students.

Can You See Out Your Contract?

Most schools, irrespective of location, will hire teachers on either a one- or two-year contract. For some people, this can be a daunting prospect as it can be seen as quite a long commitment.

One of the reasons that English teachers are in such high demand overseas is due to the high turnover of jobs in most markets. Most people aren't looking to stay abroad for the rest of their lives, or at least are not willing to stay settled in one place for too long.

Schools tend to offer yearly contracts now to avoid the conveyor belt effect, and in order to maintain some form of stability with the foreign teachers that they employ.

Ducking out on your contact or in the middle of a semester can be highly detrimental to your students, to the school and believe it or not, to yourself (for example: a wasted reference and a time gap on your CV). If you have any doubts about your commitment to teaching, then be responsible and do some voluntary teaching beforehand; or complete a classroom-based TEFL course to give yourself a taster of what's in store.

It can be unsettling for your students to just leave them in the lurch; they are counting on you - and for some children in developing countries, learning English is a great route for them to achieve something in their lives. If you provide the school with no notice and just up and leave, the students will be missing out on valuable learning time.

On the flip side, should you be unfortunate enough to find yourself in a job scam situation where the school is not fulfilling the conditions of their contract, then you are well within your rights to leave in search of more hospitable climates.

Get Some Training

Can you define the future perfect continuous tense in English and use it in a sentence? Does any average native English speaker have any idea what this even is? The point is that if you have no prior knowledge of teaching, then the chances are that teaching grammar to people could prove very tricky if you are unprepared to do so.

In addition, becoming a good teacher is something that comes with exposure to an actual classroom environment; and in the case of teaching, practice really does make perfect. If you complete an on-site TEFL training course - then expect to be challenged for that month of training - as learning how to be a successful teacher will not come to you overnight.

Holiday Time is Unpredictable

On many occasions, you will have little or no notice as to when you can take your holiday time. This makes planning trips in advance, locking in cheap airfare, and/or booking hotel rooms a difficult thing to do. Of course, weekends are always still a great chance to do some exploring and relaxing after a hectic week at work.

You might find that you simply don't have enough time mid-semester to embark on your dream trip; which is why travelling during summer breaks, or for an extended time at the end of your contract (with savings in the bank) is much more appealing to most teachers.

Communication Issues and Frequent Surprises

It has not been unknown for foreign teachers to have extra classes piled on them at the last minute, or to be told you need to do an English camp on the weekend (one day in advance), or even to your joy - that there are no classes for the remainder of this week.

The surprises can be both pleasant and unpleasant; but if you are someone who is used to having every intricate detail of your time mapped out - then just be prepared to embrace these spontaneous little jolts of surprise that are bound to come in your direction at some stage.

Further, as you will be living in a foreign country, you will find yourself up against language barriers constantly. One of the most common is when it comes to your host nation work colleagues (who are also English teachers). They will always revert back to their first language (don't forget to learn it too!); and often cut you out of the dialogue, or perhaps misinterpret what you are trying to say. This can be frustrating and counter-productive at times; but it's most probably not intentional, and it's just the way things go, so don't be too disheartened if that does happen to you.

Last But Not Least - Do You Like People? Do You Like Kids?

No matter what country you wish to work in, it's inevitable when you teach ESL abroad that you will encounter people, lots of people. Depending on your school, the amount of students in a class could range in size anywhere from one student to as many as 50 students - just think how many different personalities in one classroom that would be.

The majority of schools across the globe also come packaged with plenty of co-workers too, usually sharing a big office (with no rocks for you to hide under at nine o'clock on a Monday morning).

Much the same as any job out there, some days will be an absolute pleasure, and some days will leave you feeling frustrated. It's always important for you not to lose sight of what a great adventure you're on, and what a fantastic opportunity for you to grow as a person teaching abroad really is.

Chapter Three: Which is the Right Certification for Me?

In the world of ESL, there are three main certifications that employers will recognise. They are TEFL, TESOL, CELTA certifications. Adverts may ask for one or the other. What differentiates them and why would you choose one rather than the others? Here is the low-down including the benefits and drawbacks of each.

What is TEFL certification?

TEFL (Teaching English as a Foreign Language) is a course specifically aimed at preparing teachers for foreign language students in their own country, where English is not widely spoken. There are specific challenges involved in getting your students proficient in English. With no English speaking community nearby, there is no local immersion environment available for them to practice in. You need to give them a lot of support in the classroom. It might also help to take them online.

If you, for example, live in the US and want to travel and work from place-to-place teaching English all over the world, TEFL might be the best fit. It's also good, if you have one specific country in mind. The downside is that if you were returning home you wouldn't be able to point at your TEFL certification as your credentials for teaching immigrant communities there. But you could get work teaching foreign language speakers online.

What is the value of TESOL certification?

TESOL (Teaching English to Speakers of Other Languages) equips you for teaching English at home and abroad.

Dale from Boston runs a language institute. He trains and issues TESOL certifications at different venues around the world. His specialty is full brain and body language learning methods. Students come to him because they want to learn how to teach using his methods. That's an example of the kind of specialities and diversity available in TESOL training. In fact, a TESOL certification can be gained by many different methods from an incredible variety of service providers, each serving their own special niche. So if you have a particular methodology of language teaching you would like to learn then TESOL certification may be ideal.

An important difference between TEFL and TESOL is this: Where TEFL helps you teach abroad, TESOL is good to teach both abroad and at home. However, that diversity can be a double-edged sword. The process for earning TESOL certification is not standard so employers can't be sure of just how equipped candidates really are to teach English without asking a lot more questions.

What is CELTA?

CELTA (Certificate in Teaching English to Speakers of Other Languages) is a brand of TESOL certification. What makes it special is the quality control standards for accreditation. They are uniform for all the organisations offering it and tightly controlled. It is moderated strictly by the famous Cambridge University (English Language Assessment). This is the best recognised and most respected TESOL certification available.

To get it you'd have to do at least 20 hours of practical teaching. And the CELTA course tends to be longer than a TEFL/TESOL course. If you want your certification to get instant recognition, this is the best course to go for. The extra coaching helps you improve your teaching skills.

Now, generally TEFL is lower priced and the price of the CELTA qualification is between $1,600 to $2,000. TESOL could cost anything from $500 to $2,000, sometimes more, seldom less. But there are a few things you really have to check before you pick a school to study at. The next chapter is about the criteria for picking a good school.

But since you want to teach English abroad, the TEFL certification would be the best fit for you. Let's focus in on the TEFL certification.

More about TEFL Certification

The widespread use of English as a global language has resulted in a growing demand for English teachers abroad. It used to be that fresh college graduates backpacking their way through Thailand could boost their travel funds by teaching for a few months before resuming their journey. However, schools around the world have increasingly been calling for higher standards with regards to teachers they employ.

A TEFL certificate is now one of the most common criteria required to teach in a non-native English speaking country. Schools and recruiters will generally state that candidates are required to be a native English speaker, have a university/college degree, and have a TEFL certification. Although, that's not to say that there aren't plenty of jobs out there that won't employ non-native teachers too.

Why get TEFL certified?

On rare occasions, you may stumble across a position whereby a TEFL certificate isn't a requirement; but if you're serious about pursuing teaching ESL as career, you will want to consider this a fundamental investment to make. Like any job these days, teaching English jobs are inundated with applications from people of all different backgrounds; therefore it's important distinguish yourself from the competition.

A common misapprehension regarding teaching abroad is that it's a piece of cake. Being a native English speaker does not automatically convert into a good English teacher - nor does it mean that you're necessarily qualified to do so.

Teaching abroad is hard work, and choosing the right TEFL course will equip you with skills to effectively handle both the delights and battles faced in the classroom. It will enhance your CV, and give you a qualification that tens of thousands of schools and academies around the world will recognise.

Also, a TEFL certification will give you access to higher paid jobs with more reliable institutions. For example, if you're looking for placements in government-run schools in China, South Korea or Taiwan - then having a TEFL qualification will increase your earning capacity by up to $1,200 a year.

Above all else, it will make you a better and more confident teacher - who can give the students the quality tutoring they deserve.

Key Elements to Consider When Choosing A TEFL Certification Course

Are you new to teaching and need to learn everything such as management within the classroom, teaching grammar, theories and lesson planning? Or are you already an experienced teacher in your home country looking to join the world of teaching ESL? You'll want to consider what you're looking for from your TEFL course based on your own needs.

Give some consideration to the following factors to help you narrow down your search:

- Do you want to do an online certification or an in-classroom course?

- Should you get certified in your home country, the country you want to teach in, or a country you otherwise would like to visit?

- Can your schedule allow for a month's intensive course or can you only commit to a part-time course?

- How much money can you afford? Online courses can cost around $300 and the quality in-class courses can be in the region of $1,500.

Avoiding Bad TEFL Course Providers or Scams

You are committing time and money to your TEFL course, so do some research first to ensure avoiding any unwanted headaches down the line. All reputable TEFL providers will be accredited - if there is no accreditation, then take that as a huge red flag, and avoid this course at all costs.

Pay a visit to the TEFL provider's internet page, and see whether it is easy to contact members of the institution via their website. If they are unreachable or unresponsive - then again consider this as a warning. You should then message the alumni network at your prospective TEFL provider about the course you are interested in - this is a great opportunity before you sign up to gather further information about the course, including how it prepared previous participants to teach English abroad, and whether the program helped them to get the job they wanted.

Online TEFL Certification Courses to Consider

The benefits of online courses are that they can be completed from your laptop and at your own convenience. Typically, they cover teaching theories, grammar and lesson planning; but don't always offer any hands-on classroom training. Online courses are ideal for people who want to get a basic understanding of what it's like to teach English as a foreign language.

The course duration is also important as most teaching jobs require at least 120 hours of TEFL training (generally 100 hours of instruction and 20 hours of practicum). This is the amount of study expected of you in order to qualify and reach the international standards set by the industry to gain a professional level TEFL certification.

The following are some of my top recommendations for TEFL courses based on internet research and information gathered from teachers that I've met. There are plenty of other courses out there - so if none of the following take your fancy, be sure to have a look at what the others offer.

Teach Away Inc. (University of Toronto):

- You can choose between a 120-hour and a comprehensive 150-hour TEFL course from the University of Toronto (one of the world's top 20 universities).

- The TEFL course is self-managed and covers theory and practical classroom application of TEFL instruction for English language learners both at home and abroad.

- The 120-hour course is the most popular and it will provide you with in-depth training as you will choose from two areas of specialisation.

- The 150-hour course offers an extended core curriculum where you will choose two areas to specialise in, and complete an additional unit on teaching abroad which will prepare you for more competitive TEFL jobs.

- In addition, you will receive job assistance through Teach Away.

- Unfortunately, this course is costly at $1295 and $1495 respectively.

- One of the benefits is that this course is a partnership between a world-renowned university and an internationally renowned teacher recruitment agency: The University of Toronto provides extensive TEFL training and Teach Away Inc. strives to secure the graduates with access and assistance to leading international teaching jobs.

I-to-I TEFL

I completed my TEFL course with I-to-I, and I would recommend the course as it offers extensive training to become a TEFL certified teacher and the option to include practical classroom experience.

- I-to-I has trained over 150,000 TEFL teachers since 1994. This professional TEFL course comprises of experienced tutors and an international accreditation.

- There is interactive (online) training with personalized tutor feedback - which is accessible 24/7 via your computer, tablet or smartphone.

- Twenty hours of the course are dedicated to practical training from experienced TEFL tutors, and there will also be opportunities to practice typical TEFL scenarios with other trainees through group interaction and shared learning.

- Upon completion, you will receive free access to over 4,000 job opportunities worldwide.

- The 120-hour certificate is very reasonably priced at $275.

In-class TEFL Courses to Consider

These courses are completed in a classroom setting, and will be led by a qualified and experienced ESL instructor. Practicum is the main advantage of in-class courses and trainees can get more feel from a classroom; as opposed to online courses.

The course duration can vary depending on the provider. Typically, they range from 20-hour weekend programs, to four weeks of full-time training. Some training courses even stretch out over a period of several months.

If you opt for a course in the country you want to teach in, you'll also have the perks of getting support, and a network to find a job at the same time that you're getting certified.

The two I've selected below are based in Thailand; but you can pretty much find courses in whatever country you want to teach in.

If your aim is to teach English in Europe or the Middle East, then this type of TEFL course is strongly advised as many jobs available in these regions will request the same.

UniTEFL

- The course is based in the beautiful and culturally rich city of Chiang Mai, Thailand. UniTEFL will look after you upon arrival including: airport pick-up, accommodation, weekend excursions and teacher placements.

- The month-long TESOL/TEFL course has been created by and is run by ESL experts with a hands-on approach that includes actual classroom experience.

- The course has been validated in the United States by Fort Hays University, which entitles you to a lifetime membership to a network of 30 job centers in 20 countries.

- The certification is the only TESOL course provided in Thailand that is recognised and awarded credits from a U.S. university.

- The 120-hour course costs $1,490.

SEE TEFL

- This 120-hour course also runs for four weeks in Chiang Mai, Thailand. The courses are limited to only 18 trainees and arrangements for accommodation can be made as well.

- SEE TEFL is in its 10th year of TEFL teacher training with over 900 graduates. It is ISO 9001 accredited and is fully licensed by the Thai Ministry of Education.

- They provide authentic teaching practices with students in local schools. Training takes place in a working language school in Chiang Mai and you will gain a strong foundation in teaching fundamentals, grammar, and Thai cultural appreciation.

- After the course, you will also teach English in a classroom set-up. The places you may teach at during training include: a nursing college, a kindergarten, a primary school and a government-run university.

- The program fee starts at $1,295 and includes: study materials, reference books, testing and certification.

- The organisation also employs plenty of English teachers every year in schools within the region of Chiang Mai and Northern Thailand.

Chapter Four: How to Choose the Right School

There are a few important questions to ask when deciding which course to take. But more important than that is to pick out which school to go to. It will stand you in good stead to do your homework well. The academics offered by the school and the job search support after certification are the main factors to consider.

Here are the questions you need to ask:

How many hours will I need to study?

The right answer would be 120 hours minimum. Some TEFL and TESOL schools offer certification after a weekend, or a few weekends and sometimes without practical teaching.

A good employer wants to see a good academic standard. A minimum of 120 hours of class time with around six to 20 hours of classroom practice is good.

Classroom practice involves teaching English to real students. Shorter TEFL or TESOL certifications would usually get you to try out the methods on each other as a role play. That's not the same thing at all. Students who do not know English respond very differently to native English speaking teachers in training.

So check if the school you like provides 120 hours of coursework plus at least six hours of practicum with non-English speaking students. This doesn't mean don't do an online course. It's fine to study online as long as the academic requirements are the same and practicum is also part of the course.

Is the school properly accredited?

Obviously, the answer has to be yes, but be careful. A few schools try to look accredited using their membership with some academic association. To be a member of an association just means you have paid a membership fee. It's totally different to going through the accreditation process. If the school is accredited, great. But even so, check who it is accredited with. If the accrediting body has only existed for a few years and only has a few dozen member schools, that would be a red flag. You want to pick a school that has had a thorough review by an established regulatory body. Legitimate accreditation means the educational and professional standards of the school have been carefully reviewed by a credible and independent organisation. If that isn't obvious looking at the school, keep walking.

Who will be teaching me?

You want at least a Master's level instructor in front of the class. An instructor with a DELTA certification is also well-qualified. Your instructor must have many years of experience in the ESL environment. Some TEFL and TESOL courses are taught by mentors or tutors. Professional instructors are more expensive so TEFL courses that look too good to be true price-wise, just might be.

Must I do practical teaching myself as part of the course?

Yes, practicum (practical teaching experience in the classroom) is essential. Not all schools offer this though. If you just practice on your classmates, that doesn't count. Besides, employers will ask. If your certification didn't involve practicum, it's not complete and it won't be recognised.

How will I know what to expect from the job market?

The school should tell you. They should give you a TEFL advisor upfront to talk you through it before you spend anything. They are the best people to talk to about what you need for the job market you want to enter. They will be able to tell you what to expect in your new environment. Ask them about the cost of living, the best times to apply for work and so forth. It's a big commitment of time and money and doing research ahead of time will save you a lot of frustration and expense in the long run. If your school doesn't give that kind of support ahead of registration, you want to find someone else who will.

How will I get a job after I complete the course?

The school should help you to find work. Ask if, after the class is done, a career advisor will be available to do that. Check if you get to speak to a real person who helps you with preparing your presentation and credentials or whether they'll just send you an email with links to a few job postings. Some schools also charge for job placements. Others offer job search support only for a few weeks or months after the course is over. It can really help and it is a worthwhile question to ask.

How much does it cost?

Paying the lowest bidder is more expensive in the long run. You pay a lot more for professional and credible certification because you get professional instructors, it takes more time, it helps you prepare for the job market, and it gives you university-level education. You deserve that. You leave feeling well equipped to teach in any of 80 countries around the world. This is an investment in yourself. What you get out of it depends on what you put into it.

Cheaper TEFL/TESOL certifications cost $500, even less. They are usually less than 100 hours long. They don't include practicum. They don't offer job placement support. Or they offer dubious accreditation and less than Masters-level instructors. If they did, it would be impossible to charge such low prices. The $1,600 to $2,000 price bracket, particularly with the right brand names on average, command more respect from the job market and open doors to better working conditions.

Chapter Five: Where Can I Teach?

Whether you're a recent university graduate or you're reaching a more seasoned stage of life, there are many reasons why people are deciding to uproot and go teach English overseas. It can be to experience a new culture, save some money, seek some adventure, or just for a fresh challenge.

There are an abundance of great countries to choose from that offers a wide range of teaching jobs in all sorts of different locations. It can be hard to know where to go; so here are the top ten picks for 2017 factoring in the best experiences, pay and benefits:

South America

Argentina

They make great wine, they have exotic blue glaciers and the majestic Andes mountains. The cities are ultra-modern and richly historical at the same time. You have wildlife, rainforests and pristine beaches all in one country. What is not to love about Argentina?

Pros: Exquisite natural beauty, endless possibilities for outdoor adventure.
Cons: Not all teaching posts are paid - do research. Most jobs are in Buenos Aires where the living costs are very high. You'd probably need to live on a shoestring and you still might not break-even.

How to apply: The public schools run from March to December. Some private ones open in February. Apply at the end of February or the first week of March. If you go without a

TEFL qualification, the four-week programs available in Buenos Aires are the straightest route to a paid teaching post. But, that is also pricier.

Placement options: Government programs place you at public or private schools around Buenos Aires. If you want to work elsewhere rather, apply from inside the country.

Preferred candidates: TEFL certification required. Public schools require a teaching qualification as well.

Legal requirements: Tourist visas may last 90-180 days depending on your country of origin. It's technically illegal but schools sometimes encourage you to work on your tourist visa.

Salary: Salaries vary with higher pay available in major cities, particularly Buenos Aires. Earnings vary between $600 and $1,200. The higher end is for teachers in the big metropolis at private language schools who work full-time and really negotiate. Many hourly positions are available too, paying 30 Argentine Pesos or more per hour.

Programmes: Road2Argentina, Greenheart Travel

Brazil

Who doesn't want to explore the Amazon rainforest or the Amazon river? Rio de Janeiro has the world's most famous carnival. The people are dynamic, flamboyant, optimistic and so charismatic about it. Brazil will give you the time of your life.

Pros: Brazilian students highly esteem native English speakers as the best guides to speaking good English.

Cons: Very few lesson hours might be spaced out over an entire day with large gaps in between and transit is slow and expensive.

How to apply: Most schools look for candidates to fill teaching positions in January to start teaching in March. It is best to apply from inside the country.

Placement options: Hundreds of language schools demand English Language Instructors to teach business English to business professionals.

Preferred candidates: Bachelor's degree preferred. TEFL certification essential and at least some teaching experience.

Legal requirements: It is illegal to work on a tourist visa, although most do. A work visa requires that you be sponsored by a company/school and they would usually require a commitment of a year or more.

Salary: Monthly $1,400 to $1,600. At a school you would earn $25 per hour teaching, but teaching privately you would earn $50 per hour. English for technical specialisations like business, engineering, law and medicine command higher rates.

Programmes: BrazilianGringo, Come Teach English in Brazil

Chile

Are you into skiing or exploring the incredible diversity of nature? Chile has the majestic Andes mountain range plus the famous archipelagos of Easter Island. The most breathtaking lightning storms crackle across the Atacama desert. Chile has so much to offer.

Pros: Modern cities with stable economy and so much to see and do especially if you are into outdoor adventure sports. Chilean students love getting involved in the lessons.

Cons: It is very difficult to get a job offer from outside the country. Living expenses are very high. Employment relations are very poor. Some view language institutes as get-rich-quick schemes for unscrupulous entrepreneurs. There is a lot of bureaucratic red tape to deal with.

How to apply: Apply late February and March, when the school year begins.

Placement options: At universities and schools, a four-year Bachelor's degree is required, plus TEFL certification. A BA (Education) or B.Ed is preferred. Alternatively you could join a language institute. If you don't have that, you could join a private program that links native English speakers with local schools and businesses wanting their employees to improve in English.

Preferred candidates: Native English speakers accepted. B.Ed graduates with TEFL certification and teaching experience preferred.

Legal requirements: If you are offered a contract (good for you) you can get appropriate work permits[1]. Otherwise, work on a tourist visa and cross the Argentine border every three months to renew it.

Salary: You could get $900 to $1,200 per month. Language institutes pay $4 to $8 per hour. Private lessons command $9 per hour. Depending on your credentials you could negotiate higher.

Programmes: CIEE Teach Abroad, i-to-i, teachingChile

Colombia

Thirty years ago, it would have been impossible to teach in Colombia as it was thriving with drug cartels and political turmoil. Today however, it boasts one of Latin America's top job markets for teaching English: with an expanding economy, idyllic beaches and lush rainforests. Larger cities such as Bogotá and Medellín offer an abundance of teaching positions;

---

[1] Under the Chilean boletas system (governments personal invoice system) the government takes 10% of every paycheck and gives it back the following May.

not to mention a rich culture, colourful markets and roaring nightlife scenes.

Pros: There are plenty of teaching positions in private institutions, and the Colombian government announced positions for foreign teachers in public schools across the country. Moving to Colombia also presents you with the fantastic opportunity to brush up on your Spanish language skills.

Cons: Some positions will be available to you only if you apply from within the country.

How to apply: November to January are the best months for applying for work. It is best to find a school yourself from inside the country but if you have very strong qualifications you would be able to apply through a program and get a placement ahead of your arrival.

Placement options: Private international schools require a few years experience and a TEFL certification from native speakers. Language institutes only ask for a Bachelor's degree. Public schools may offer co-teacher posts.

Preferred candidates: Generally the requirements are native speaker, Bachelor's degree, TEFL certification and at least one year of teaching experience.

Legal requirements: It is possible, through teaching programs, to get a work visa but most work on their three-month tourist visas.

Salary: Private lessons command $12 to $30 per hour. Average salary is $900 to $1,500 per month depending on the school and your credentials.

Programmes: World Teach, Internships Colombia

Ecuador

Check out the Galápagos Islands which has the greatest biodiversity in the world. Waterfalls, wildlife and exquisite mountains and volcanoes dot the Ecuadorian landscape. The history of its major cities stretch back at least 500 years and its ruins are millennia old. It's absolutely worth a visit.

Pros: The food is fresh and diverse, the cost of living is very low. The natural beauty is abundant.
Cons: Emails are ignored, internet sites are often offline so looking online for work may be asking too much.

How to apply: Apply in February to March and July to August from inside the country.
Placement options: The most secure and best paying work is at university. Schools and language institutes are generally laid-back. Private lessons are the most lucrative option. Your students would be business professionals.
Preferred candidates: Native English speakers get preference. Bachelor's degree is preferred. TEFL certification required.

Legal requirements: Work visa. Come as a tourist, get a job offer and then convert your tourist visa to a work permit.
Salary: Average salary $500 to $700 per month. Without certifications you could be hired at $3 to $5 per hour. With experience, a degree and a TEFL certification, you would earn much more.
Programmes: Cuenca Highlife, Language Corps

Central America

Costa Rica

Costa Rica, or the "Rich Coast" as it translates, is becoming an increasingly popular destination for ESL teachers. This is mainly due to its rapidly developing economy, tropical rainforests, active volcanoes, and beautiful coastlines. The locals are famous for their "pure life" spirit, and a widespread tourism industry has caused a demand for locals needing to learn English.

Pros: Living a laid-back lifestyle in paradise and for a low cost of living.
Cons: The low cost of living is relative, as you will probably only break-even with what you earn.

How to apply: Apply all year round, from inside the country.
Placement options: Contracts are 6 or 12 months long. Students would be business professionals.
Preferred candidates: Bachelor's degree is preferred. TEFL certification required.

Legal requirements: Work visa or Independent Contractor Licence.
Salary: $800 to $1,000 per month.
Programmes: Frontier Gap, International TEFL Academy

Europe

Czech Republic

Located in the centre of Europe, the Czech Republic is a country that offers a medieval feel with its array of castles, cobblestone streets and traditional villages. In addition, bustling cities such as Prague and Brno, supply a large amount of the teaching jobs.

Pros: The central location makes it an excellent base to explore the rest of Europe from.
Cons: It's difficult for those looking to get a job in a public school.

How to apply: Apply from inside the country in September or January.
Placement options: Contracts are 10 or 12 months long. Students are either children or business professionals.
Preferred candidates: Bachelor's degree is preferred. TEFL certification required.

Legal requirements: Enter on a tourist visa, get a job offer and convert that to a work visa unless you have EU citizenship.
Salary: $1,000 to $1,300 per month.
Programmes: The Language House, Language Corps

France

France is a dream for the romantic, the reader, the art lover, the gourmet and anyone with appreciation for history. France has history documented in its landscape stretching back to the Roman Empire.

Pros: You would be teaching business professionals who are determined to learn and improve.
Cons: Starting costs are high, no airfare, housing or any other subsidies are available.

How to apply: Apply in September or January from inside the country.
Preferred candidates: Bachelor's degree required. B.Ed preferred. Native English speakers or EU citizens. TEFL certification required.

Legal requirements: France accepts applicants on a student visa. After landing a job offer the visa can be converted to a work permit in the case of government programs.
Salary: Average salary $1,050 to $2,000 per month
Programmes: Higher Education, CIEP

Hungary

Hungary is an absolutely diverse country teeming with people from every corner of the globe. It's major cities are very modern and advanced but at the same time rich in history and heritage. It is also a great launch pad for exploring the rest of both Eastern and Western Europe.

Pros: Do your interview online and land a job before you arrive.
Cons: No support for housing, airfare, transport, etc.

How to apply: Hiring season is September or January.
Placement options: Contracts are generally 10 to 12 months. You would most likely be teaching either professional people or children.
Preferred candidates: Besides TEFL certification, a four-year Bachelor's degree is required.

Legal requirements: You may apply with a tourist visa and convert that to work visa when you have a contract.
Salary: Average salary $600 to $800 per month.
Programmes: CETP, Language Corps

Spain

There is a plethora of reasons why people choose to live and teach in Spain. There really is something for everybody: ranging from the vibrant cities of Barcelona and Madrid; to the party island hot-spots of Ibiza and Tenerife; or the more chilled, picturesque Alicante and Bilbao. There are plenty of teaching jobs available, especially during the main hiring seasons in January and September.

Pros: There are a lot of school positions available.
Cons: The pay is not as high as in certain Asian countries or the Middle East, but you will still be able to break-even. Also, there are trickier work visa conditions for non-EU citizens.

How to apply: Apply in late September or early October, or in January from inside the country.
Placement options: Placement in a government program may allow you to land a job after an online interview. You would primarily be teaching business professionals.
Preferred candidates: A Bachelor's degree is preferred but not required, TEFL certification is required.

Legal requirements: A tourist, work or student visa or an EU citizenship will be enough to allow you to work.
Salary: Salaries range from $900 to $2,000 per month depending on the school and your qualifications.
Programmes: CIEE, MECD

Middle East

United Arab Emirates

Perhaps not everyone's first choice; however, if you're feeling adventurous, some of the highest-paid ESL teaching positions are offered here. It's a diverse nation - with an already populous expat community. If you want to explore deserts, lakes and oceans; or if you desire a taste of luxury, then this is the place for you.

Pros: Huge salary, no taxes, and no shortage of markets and shopping malls.
Cons: They will only hire certified and experienced English teachers - so this is not an option for recent university graduates.

How to apply: Apply online all year round.
Placement options: You would either be teaching business professionals at language schools and universities or children at private or public schools.
Preferred candidates: A Masters degree is preferred. Bachelor's degree and TEFL certification is required. At least a few years of teaching experience required as well.

Legal requirements: Secure your work visa in advance.
Salary: $1,800 to $5,000 per month.
Programmes: Teach Away, Footprints Recruiting

Saudi Arabia

Saudi Arabia is an ideal stepping stone to explore Europe and Asia as airfares are very reasonable. The country is home to a huge and diverse expat community and you are sure to meet fascinating people from all over the world.

Pros: Highly developed infrastructure. You could save $800 or more with the difference between your cost of living and your average salary. Free housing and airfare is often included.

Cons: Very strict security controls, very high standards for applicants both in terms of academic requirements and minimum experience required.

How to apply: Apply at any time of the year but May to August are best. You can land a job over a Skype interview in advance.

Placement options: Typical contracts are 12 months long.

Preferred candidates: A Bachelor's degree is required, a Master degree is preferred.

Legal requirements: Obtain your work permit in advance.

Salary: Monthly average $2,600 to $4,000 tax free.

Programmes: British Council, i-to-i

Kuwait

Kuwait doesn't have any of the over-commercialised bling you see in other Gulf countries. It will give you an authentic Arab experience in the best way, nothing extreme about it. Besides it's rich history remains more or less intact and easy to explore.

Pros: The cost of living is well below the average salary so you can save $850 or more per month for exploring during downtime. Housing is generally also covered.

Cons: High entry requirements with Masters degrees preferred.

How to apply: Apply year round, online but especially in May to August.

Placement options: You would most likely be teaching either business professionals or children on a 12-month contract.
Preferred candidates: Master's degrees with documented experience teaching ESL in a foreign environment.

Legal requirements: Secure your work visa in advance.
Salary: $1,800 to $3,700 per month, tax-free
Programmes: Teach Away, GoOverseas

Asia

Thailand

Thailand generally draws in a lot of new and younger teachers as no previous teaching experience is required. That's not to say that there aren't any older teachers here because there are many - especially those who seem set to retire in this beautiful country. It's the gateway to Asia, and it has a low cost of living.

Pros: Hot weather, tropical beaches, delicious local food, friendly locals and a party atmosphere.
Cons: A large amount of students in the classroom (up to 45) and a flimsy education system.

Salary: $1,000 for public school jobs and up to $1,400 for private institution jobs in Bangkok.
Programmes: SEE TEFL, GoTEFL Thailand

Cambodia

Cambodia has survived mass genocide, poverty and the most gory brutality and emerged as a spirited and optimistic nation, with beautiful cities and unspoilt beaches. It's an inspiring place to visit.

Pros: Lower restrictions for non-native English speakers
Cons: No airfares or housing subsidies are available.

How to apply: Apply from inside Cambodia all year round.
Placement options: Contracts are typically 6 or 12 months.
Preferred candidates: Bachelor's degree preferred.

Legal requirements: Your tourist visa can be converted to a work visa after landing a contract.
Salary: Average salary is $900 to $1,100 per month.
Programmes: Hunt ESL, i-to-i

Vietnam

Vietnam has a thriving ESL teaching market that offers good salaries and a low cost of living. Get lost in the highlands of Sapa; or experience the hustle and bustle of Hanoi; check out the colourful street markets in Ho Chi Minh City; and gaze into the Mekong River.

Pros: Teachers can bank over $500 in savings after expenses.
Cons: Schools generally require native English speakers, a university degree and a TEFL certificate.

How to apply: Apply from inside Vietnam all year round.
Placement options: Contracts are typically 12 months.
Preferred candidates: Bachelor's degree required.

Legal requirements: Work visa.
Salary: $1,400 to $2,100 per month depending on the school and your qualifications.
Programmes: Smaller Earth, AMA

China

There's an estimated 300 million people in China learning English - so naturally the job market is wide open. Regardless of where you go, there will be fantastic job opportunities - especially in the major cities of Beijing and Shanghai.

Pros: Free housing, free lunches, completion bonuses and airfare reimbursement.

Cons: Polluted cities and bad placements. Remember to always do your research first!

How to apply: Apply online ahead of time and land the contract in China any time of the year.
Placement options: Contracts are typically 6 to 12 months.
Preferred candidates: Bachelor's degree preferred, TEFL certification required.

Legal requirements: Work visa.
Salary: $1,000 to $3,000 per month depending on the school and your qualifications.
Programmes: ESL Café, Immerqi

Japan

The wonders of Japan really need no introduction. This island-nation is filled with high-rise cities, imperial palaces, majestical national parks, and copious temples. If you're seeking neon lights and pop culture, then head to Tokyo. However, if a slice of history is more your thing, then check out the temples and gardens of Kyoto.

Pros: The food, people, culture, history and natural beauty.
Cons: A high cost of living, especially in Tokyo. No downtimes.

How to apply: Any time of the year, online.
Placement options: Contracts are typically 12 months.
Preferred candidates: Native speakers with Bachelor's degree minimum and TEFL certification plus at least some teaching experience.

Legal requirements: Work visa.
Salary: $1,700 to $4,000 per month depending on the school and your qualifications.
Programmes: GABA Corporation, JET

Taiwan

The cost of living is low and the climate is temperate. Taiwan has amazing variety of natural wonders in close proximity. Plus, it boasts super-advanced infrastructure.

Pros: You can apply for and land and job in advance. It also allows you to save $500 per month. The medical care system is accessible and crime is very low.
Cons: Racism, pollution and very high startup costs.

How to apply: Apply after Chinese Lunar New Year and during July to August.
Placement options: 12 month contracts are typical.
Preferred candidates: Native English speakers, Bachelor's degree required.

Legal requirements: Work visa to be issued in advance.
Salary: Average salary is $1,400 to $2,000 per month.
Programmes: AEON, NOVA

South Korea

South Korea is a super-modern country yet it still manages to keep a historical feel to it. There are approximately 25,000 foreign English teachers in Korea, so there is no shortage of positions available.

Pros: It's possible to bank up to $1,500 a month after expenses.
Cons: A lot of the private academies have their fair share of horror stories - so again, do your research first.

How to apply: Anytime, online.
Placement options: 12 month contracts are typical.

Preferred candidates: Native English speakers, Bachelor's degree required.

Legal requirements: Work visa to be issued in advance.
Salary: $1,900 to $2,500 per month.
Programmes: ESL Café, EPIK

The World is Your Oyster...

These are just a handful of nations around the world that offer incredible opportunities to work and live in a different country. Whatever country you choose, you are in for a fun ride. Do your research and make a decision on what suits your needs best as many countries have varying perks to them.

PART II - Land a Job

Chapter Six: How to Prepare the Perfect CV

Your resumé or CV will be the first point of contact you have with potential employers, so it's important to make a good first impression.

Below are some valuable pointers and a proven CV template to help you land the perfect teaching job overseas.

Are You Qualified?

Experience and qualifications are the two key components of your CV, but the precise requirements will vary depending on your desired destination.

In lots of countries, a degree is required to obtain a visa; often with a TEFL certification requested in addition. As mentioned previously, some countries in Europe and the Middle East will require a degree, CELTA or Trinity TESOL certification, and teaching experience. Don't fret, however; there are a variety of countries in Asia and South America that don't require any previous teaching experience.

Remember if you do want to work in a country that requires previous teaching experience, there are ways to bolster your CV credentials. You could first do some one-on-one tutoring; online teaching; volunteering; an on-site TEFL course with classroom practice; or you could opt for a country that doesn't require any prior teaching experience, and use it as a stepping stone.

Recommended CV Format

Look for the most specific requirements in the job description and make them standout in your CV. Aim to keep your CV brief; but don't forget you're marketing yourself as an English teacher, who is prepared to move abroad, serve the needs of the school that hires you, and effectively teach their students.

Therefore, be sure to highlight the skills that you've acquired over the years, such as: working with children, interpersonal, training, presenting and/or time management skills. Don't forget to provide your background in living overseas; as it demonstrates both your independence and adaptability.

If you're not a native English speaker, then add any work or academic testing that you have previously done to enhance your chances and exhibit your fluency in the language.

CV TEMPLATE

Contact Details

Add your full name, date of birth and nationality. Also, make sure you include your email address - as employers are most likely to contact you this way in the initial stages.

Photo

Most schools or institutions will want you to include a photograph of yourself on your CV; but perhaps avoid putting up any frowning passport pictures. Your picture should still be professional, and you should be smartly dressed. Further, you want to give an insight to your personality, and you'll want employers to think you look like good teacher material - so don't forget to smile.

Profile

This is your chance to summarise yourself, your aims, and your ambitions. Steer clear of the standard "I'm a great team player" spiel; and instead concentrate on what you can bring to the table as a teacher, why you want to teach in that country, and if you can personalise it as to why you want to work at a particular school as it will show that you've done your research.

Qualifications/Employment History

Provide details here of your university, your major, the dates of study and your degree class. If you have completed a TEFL certification; you should also incorporate this at this stage.

List your previous jobs, starting with the most recent or most relevant (if you do already have teaching experience). You can add some bullet points and give a short overview of the work duties that you performed, and tailor them so they are relevant to the job that you're applying for.

Other Information/Interests

If there is anything else you consider relevant to the job, then put it in here. For example: what transferable skills do you possess - have you tutored any young students, or given any presentations? Think about how your experiences can be applied to a teaching job - have you completed any IT courses or do your hobbies include reading or travelling? Anything that shows you are equipped to be an effective teacher should be included.

References

Have two references readily available, or write 'references available on request' in this section of your CV. Again you don't need to have teaching specific references, just two previous employers of any job nature will suffice; or if you're a recent graduate, you can use a university tutor.

Proofread!

Don't send out your CV before you have thoroughly examined it for spelling or grammatical mistakes. You're applying to teach English to non-native speakers, so it's imperative that you get this correct, or you could fall at the first hurdle in terms of getting a teaching job. Get someone else to have a look over it for you, and when you're certain it's all in order, you can start sending it out to prospective employers.

Creating the perfect TEFL CV is one of the first and most important steps to seeing you on your way to landing your dream teaching job.

Chapter Seven: How to Apply for a TEFL Position

Now, with the perfect CV in hand, here is how to look for a job. If you're planning to make the jump into teaching English abroad, you need to familiarise yourself with the best ways to apply for ESL jobs. The following methods are all frequently used by teachers in order to find teaching positions:

Options Available When Applying for ESL Teaching Jobs Overseas

- Apply online and direct to the school
- Apply in person
- Apply through a recruiter
- Social networking/ word of mouth
- All of the above

The job hunt will differ from country to country - this has been taken into account here to ensure that all the above methods are taken into account regarding how you can secure your ideal teaching job.

Route 1: Applying Online and Direct to the School

Regions: Asia, Eastern Europe, and the Middle East.

Positives: You'll have a job secured before you set off.
Negatives: There is danger of poor job quality or scams.

Countries in Asia, Eastern Europe and the Middle East have a widespread need for teachers; therefore, schools are willing to carry out interviews online, as opposed to in person. There are numerous ESL websites that offer a job board, with a wide range of daily advertisements from various schools and ESL recruitment companies.

The next step is to click on a job advertisement that takes your fancy and apply by sending across your CV and a cover letter. Alternatively, some schools or institutions will have their own application forms for you to fill out and submit.

It's important to have soft copies of your degree, passport and TEFL certificate - as most ads will request copies of the same. It will also be advantageous to have a professional-looking head shot photograph for the CV itself, and some pictures of yourself preferably in a teaching environment to accompany your application as a whole.

Keep in mind when you're submitting your applications that you'll be coming up against different time zones, and language barriers - so just be understanding, and don't panic if you don't get any immediately favourable results. If you fulfill the job criteria then chances are you will start to hear back from applications fairly soon.

There will always be an element of uncertainty when committing to an overseas teaching job as you won't have had chance to view the school, or meet co-workers face to face.

At no stage should a school request any upfront payments from you, so be aware of scams such as these. Any school worth noting will have a professional contract drawn up for your perusal, and for you to consider the conditions contained therein such as: salary, work hours, duration of contract, and the termination procedures. It is always recommended to ask if you can contact a foreign teacher who currently works at the school so you can pick their brains.

Applying online is a great route to take as it eliminates the uncertainty that follows from making off the cuff moves abroad, with little or no money to your name. You can select what region you wish to work in and send out a bunch of applications. After that you can do some online research on the city, and the job to see what suits you best once you've started to receive some offers.

Always remember you're not bound to your contract in blood. If things do start to turn sour, you can always find a new job and change schools just the same as any other job back home.

Route 2: Applying Whilst in Your Country of Choice

Regions: Applies anywhere, though it's more common in Europe and South America.

Positives: A greater chance of getting employed and the advantage of viewing the school in person.
Negatives: Making a move abroad without a guaranteed job.

The second option to finding ESL jobs is by applying locally, and when you're already in your desired destination. You may have already decided which country you want to work in; or you may want to travel to a few countries before you start work, and scout out which option feels best for you.

Applying this way is less secure in the sense that you won't have a job lined up before you set off from your home country. You will however, discover more positions this way, and both you and the school will reap all the benefits of a face-to-face meeting.

Openings at language academies often come up all year around, and often relatively last minute. Consequently, teachers sometimes find their way into full time work by filling in as a substitute teacher for a short period of time, or simply by luck of being in the right place at the right time.

In South America, it's tricky to find positions online or before you arrive, so a bit of spontaneity is required by journeying to the continent first, and applying when you're there. In both Asia and Europe, teaching jobs online are plentiful, but some jobs give preference to applicants who are already in the country.

There are of course risks attached to applying for ESL jobs in person. It requires you to purchase a plane ticket and budget, perhaps, a month's worth of living costs while you search for work. If you are serious about teaching though, the benefits of applying locally will almost certainly outweigh the risks.

Not yet TEFL certified? Apply for an onsite course in a particular region. If you're not already TEFL qualified, you could complete the in-class course in the region that you would like to teach. It allows you to spend four weeks getting acquainted with your new surroundings; and it also gives you a further option of looking for jobs locally yourself, which gives you even more chance of landing the right job for you.

This option will be a bit more costly in comparison to completing an online TEFL course, but if you can afford the investment, it will provide you with security before you embark from your country of origin.

Route 3: Apply Through an ESL Recruitment Agency

Regions: Asia and the Middle East.

Positives: You'll have a job secured before you set off.
Negatives: Unprofessional recruiters.

It's routine in countries such as China, Taiwan, South Korea, Saudi Arabia, and the UAE for the schools to hire teachers via a recruitment agency. Some of the larger ESL agencies are as follows:

- Footprints Recruiting (Worldwide)
- Greenheart Travel (Worldwide)
- Reach to Teach (Worldwide)
- Teach Away (Worldwide)
- Teaching Nomad (China, Middle East)
- Gold Star TEFL (China)
- GABA Corporation (Japan)
- Adventure Teaching (South Korea)
- Korean Horizons (South Korea)
- Media Kids Academy (Thailand)

Most agencies will require you to have a three- or four-year university degree, a TEFL certificate and potentially, some form of previous teaching experience.

Essentially, applying this way involves sending all your documents to a recruiter, who will in turn find you a job. They will contact you initially to conduct a short Skype interview, where they will ask you some basic questions. A benefit with this route is that you can eradicate some of the job hunt headaches, rely on someone else to find a job for you, and in the majority of cases, very promptly too.

There still remains a slight element of risk (similarly to applying direct to a school); in that no face-to-face meeting or tour of your school will be held before you accept a position. So again, just do some homework on both your school or recruiter, and make sure the terms of your contract are readily available to you before you put pen to paper.

A lot of agencies will work with credible schools, for which they regularly place teachers. On the flip side, some recruiters will be more concerned with commission; and will therefore place you wherever they can, so potentially at an unsavoury establishment. So be weary of this and use your better judgment.

Furthermore, recruitment agencies generally charge a placement fee direct from the school, and some will ask for a commission from the teacher. It may be worth it if you land a good position, but make sure that the commission/fee system is agreed in advance. Media Kids in Thailand for example, will take a cut of your salary; but they will provide assistance for things like visas and work permits.

Government Programs in Public Schools

Much like ESL recruitment agencies, certain countries participate in government-run schemes in order to place teachers, such as Japan (JET Programme), and South Korea (TALK and EPIK). Usually, you won't get to choose where you will be situated within the country. They can be very competitive and in places like Korea, they have even cut the amount of jobs that are available.

Route 4: Facebook and Word of Mouth

Regions: All over the world.

Positives: Recommended to you by a trustworthy source.
Negatives: Not knowing anybody in the teaching field of work.

Put yourself out there, do some networking, and make some connections. Join TEFL groups on Facebook, and you'll see that jobs are posted daily throughout the pages.

Additionally, speak to friends or friends of friends who may already be teaching ESL overseas - they may be able to put you in contact with their employer.

Even when you do start working at a job, you should always keep your options open as a more suitable opportunity may arise. ESL teaching jobs are available year round and all over the world - people leave early, or go off to travel after their job is complete, so there could always be a better job opportunity waiting right around the corner.

Route 5: A Combination of All of the Above Methods

The best advice is to utilise all of the methods available to you, until you find your perfect ESL teaching job. They are all available for you to take advantage of - so be brave and send out your CVs and give it a try. You may be surprised at just how many responses you will receive.

Chapter Eight: Preparing For a Skype Interview

If you're applying to teach English abroad - you will, at some stage be required to complete a Skype video interview with a recruiter, and/or a representative from your potential school.

For anyone who's not had a Skype interview before, here are some useful tips on how to ace the interview process:

Your Skype Information

The first items the interviewer will see prior to the interview are: your Skype ID, profile, photo, and status. You'll need to make sure these are all in order and of a professional nature; or create a separate Skype account for professional matters if necessary.

Technical Readiness

Become Skype savvy, and ensure that you have accepted or sent the relevant contact request so that your interviewer is not kept waiting (take note of time zone differences as well). It's recommended that you're online and prepared to go around 15 minutes before the agreed time of the interview. Check that your webcam and microphone are in working order, and that your internet connection is stable.

First Impressions

Look and dress smart, exactly the same as you would if you were attending the interview in person. The background area will be in eye-shot for the interviewer - so it should be tidy, and there should be nothing inappropriate in sight; position yourself with a plain wall behind you if it's possible. You'll want to make sure you're in a well-lit area as well. Also, it is essential that the surrounding area is quiet to ensure that you can communicate smoothly.

Be Confident

It can be tricky if you overthink this point, but try to be as natural and confident as you can in front of the camera. Ensure that you keep eye contact, smile and project yourself well to the interviewer. Your confidence will grow with each Skype interview that you do.

Don't Forget It's a Job Interview

Fulfilling all the job criteria does not automatically mean you'll be offered the job. It's likely that there will be other candidates being screened for the same position, so remember to show enthusiasm and demonstrate that you do want it.

Do Your Research

Prior to the interview, find out some of the basics about the job you're applying for. If you're going through a recruiter, then ask them some questions about the school and what the job entails.

Sell Yourself and Know What's On Your CV

The interviewer will already have a copy of your CV to hand; however, they will still want to hear about your experiences from you personally, so be prepared to reiterate them during the process.

If you're worried that you have no previous teaching experience, then utilise other qualities you have gained to your advantage. For example, explain to them how your TEFL course training equipped you to feel confident in the classroom, and how it has put you in good stead to deal productively with students. Better yet, go out there and get some experience: do some volunteering with children in your spare time and boost your CV credentials.

Here are some examples of standard questions that are typically asked during Skype interview process:

- Talk about you and your plans for teaching overseas
- Why are you applying for a position in...?
- What makes this school/institution more appealing to you than others?
- What qualities do you have that will make you a good teacher?
- Talk about a difficult situation at work/in a classroom and how you resolved it
- Talk about a good lesson that you have planned?

At the end of the interview, you will more than likely be asked if you have any questions yourself. Be sure to have a couple of questions ready as this is also a good chance for you to demonstrate your keenness, and to find out anything else you would like to know about the job.

Chapter Nine: Get Work Teaching English Online

There are a vast number of platforms where you would be able to find work teaching online. Some are semi private tutoring platforms where students connect to individual tutors. Others require a certain number of hours, a certain level of availability or just a certain level of credentials. Here are a few options you can look into.

Private teaching online

Topica Native

It's a Vietnamese program to connect native English speakers with English language learners using Google Class and adaptive learning technology. To get in, teaching experience is preferable but not required. The time you teach is generally up to you as classes begin Eastern Time at 8AM and end at 11PM, each class lasts 45 minutes. As long as you have a quiet environment and a stable internet connection, you can teach. The pay scale varies significantly according to experience.

Preply

This is not a traditional teaching platform in that it connects individuals. You as a teacher can directly approach students who have expressed the need to learn what you teach. Students request tutoring on a topic and you as the tutor can respond. This is a US-based company. They prefer candidates who are comfortable speaking the students language as well as being a native English speaker but they do not demand TEFL certification.

Online Language Schools

Lingoda

All English teachers get one-on-one training time with language learners. Lingoda provides all the learning materials as well as libraries for particular areas of interest such as vocabulary, pronunciation or grammar issues you might want to give your student extra support with. The hours and times of work is up to you. You would need MS Office skills and would be paid per hour but the rate depends on your credentials.

RareJob

Rarejob is an online Japanese English Language school employing Filipinos. You would use Skype to teach, and a webcam is recommended so you would need a good internet connection to work here. They do not need a knowledge of Japanese but they only employ tutors who live in the Philippines.

VerbalPlanet

This is a teaching platform that does require qualifications, proven experience and credentials. Payments are made through PayPal and students pay a booking fee to the site in addition to the rate you charge as a teacher. Lessons are 45 minutes long and students can only book your time in the time slots you offer them.

BuddySchool

Students pay for lessons when they book, which guarantees your income - paid through PayPal. You put up your profile, show when you are available on their calendar and students from anywhere in the world interested in learning from you will contact you.

learnship.de

This is a corporate online German language school. It is aimed at executives keen to broaden their linguist capabilities. They offer English as a Second Language specialisation in medicine, engineering, law and so forth. They put great store on their teaching methodologies and in addition to the credentials they require from applicants, they also insist on further online teacher training and service a big percentage of DAX (German stock exchange) listed public companies.

For a job board showing vacancies for online teaching positions you may want to take a look at: https://eslauthority.com/teach/online/jobs/

Chapter Ten: Questions You Need to Ask Before You Accept a Job

It's an exciting feeling when your hard work pays off and you start to see job offers coming in. It can however, be tempting to get carried away as you are one step closer to packing your suitcase and moving abroad.

Before you do accept a job offer, it's crucial to fully research all the conditions of the position by asking important questions during the interview and subsequent contract negotiations. Making relevant inquiries can ultimately be the difference between landing a good or a bad TEFL placement.

Here are a variety of questions you should pose before signing a contract:

Teacher Duties

- What procedures does the school have in place regarding the curriculum, lessons, and lesson planning?
- Do teachers have to prepare any reports, or do any additional grading?
- Are there any additional responsibilities for teachers?
- What dress code is expected of teachers?

Work Hours

- What's the maximum hours in a day that you will have to work, and up until what time?
- Are there any extra hours of work expected of you? If yes, will you be reimbursed for these?
- What is the duration of each class?
- How many classes will you to teach each week?

- How many days a week will you work?
- Will you have to teach any English camps (summer or winter)? Is this obligatory?
- Are there any additional work meetings?

Students

- What level are the students?
- How many students are there per class?
- What's the total number of students at the school?
- Are there any disciplinary practices in place at the school?

Current Teachers

- How many foreign teachers are there?
- Can they give you contact details of a foreign teacher at the school for you to talk to?
- Have any of the teachers (past or current) renewed their contact?

Visas

- What is the visa process? Will the school assist you with this?
- What type visa will you enter the country on?
- How long will it take for you to obtain a visa?
- Who will pay for the visa?

Flights

- Is there a reimbursement for your airfare? When will you receive the airfare?
- Will they provide any airport pick-up?

Holidays

- How many days holiday a year will you receive?
- Are holidays paid or unpaid?
- When can you take holiday time?

Money

- What is the overall salary? Are there any taxes or deductions to be factored in?
- Is the salary range dependent upon qualifications, or how is it worked out?
- When do you get paid?
- Are there any bonuses for completion of the contract?
- Will the money be deposited into a bank account?
- Will the school provide any assistance with opening a bank account?
- Will there be overtime pay or allowance?
- Do you have to pay anything towards a pension plan, and/or medical insurance? Does the school make any contributions to this, and are there any documents to prove so?
- Can you earn any extra money outside of school hours doing private tutoring?

Housing

- Will the school provide housing, or is there a housing allowance?
- How much are utility bills on average?
- Is the housing close to the school, or will you need to commute?
- Is it shared housing?

A lot of the aforementioned points will not be included within the contract. It's imperative that you speak to your recruiter, a current foreign teacher, and the school to ascertain the answers to these questions; and if need be, to negotiate a better deal for yourself. If you are in any doubt, or something doesn't seem quite right - don't forget that there are plenty of other teaching positions out there that you can consider.

Chapter Eleven: What to Pack before You Leave

Packing your suitcase to move overseas can be an alarming task when considering how many things you need to take with you. Review the information provided below to ensure you have remembered everything you need to take well in advance of your departure.

We enjoy a high standard of living in the western world so you will want to take some home comforts with you; but not so much that it hampers your new adventure, nor your luggage capacity.

Essentials - Before You Arrive

- Documents (passport and birth certificate), and copies of each document.
- Documents (TEFL certificate, degree diploma, criminal record), and copies of each document.
- Research the visa process and requirements of your destination, and the costs involved.
- Are notarised and/or apostilled degree diplomas/criminal records required?
- Run a Google search "what is it like to live and teach in...?" Check articles online, or expat forums about the living and teaching conditions in the country you're considering.
- Research the recruiters and schools before you accept any position.
- Check your contract terms thoroughly: salary, medical insurance, housing, termination details.
- Have you requested details on your accommodation and the proximity of it to your school?
- Extra passport photos (around a dozen).

- Expiry of your current passport (some countries have a six-month passport validity requirement for entry).
- Airline tickets and itinerary (to provide to your school for reimbursement).
- Get a contact number and address for someone at your school.
- International driving license (you may want to purchase or rent a car/motorbike abroad).
- Money - how much will you need for your first month?
- Saving money - how much to send back home each month?
- Managed debts back home (student loans or credit cards)?
- Do you need any vaccinations?
- Research cultural do's and do not's - in Thailand it is considered rude to touch somebody's head and in Korea people bow to greet each other.

Living Items - For During Your Stay

- Clothing - suitable for the classroom and suitable for the climate/travelling.
- Are your personal items going to be secure in your apartment: passport, credit cards, and laptop?
- Luggage tags.
- Photos of your loved ones.
- Contact information of your family and friends.
- Luxury items - camera, music, books, etc.
- Writing journal.
- An electrical adapter to charge your devices.
- Toiletries/hygiene/cosmetic products (not always available overseas).
- Language phrase book.

Classroom Necessities

- Writing paper, pens, etc. - if you're unsure whether your school provides the same.
- Any ESL teaching resources that you may have: lesson activities, lesson plans and resource books.
- Research ESL websites for useful classroom activities beforehand.

PART III - Succeeding as an ESL Teacher

Chapter Twelve: Private Tutoring Abroad

As you get into the swing of things in your new environment, you might have time between classes as a TEFL teacher abroad. In fact, at the average rate of 20 hours a week of work, you would most likely have quite some extra time. If you want to use that to earn some extra money, programs for private tutoring are also available. There are camps such as The English Camp Company in Rome and homestay programs through Cultural Homestay International (CHI) in Brazil, China, all over Europe and other parts of the world. AngloBridge is another example of a forum for finding private students to tutor. It is a one-on-one meet up for English language students in Eastern Europe.

Aside from starting right online to pick up private students, you may find students through your teaching post who would prefer to be taught privately by you. As you make yourself at home in your new environment you will meet many people, and hopefully make many new friends. In time you may be able to earn your entire fee straight from students with no school commissions off the top.

Chapter Thirteen: The Key Qualities Needed to Become a Successful ESL Teacher Abroad

There are a vast variety of skill sets that are needed as a teacher that won't just appear overnight - these will only be acquired by: putting in time and effort, learning from your mistakes, and practicing your job technique. It is important to consider what methods of teaching are required in the classroom environment to really make a difference to the students' development.

Being an ESL teacher really does give you a great sense of job satisfaction when you start to witness first-hand that your students are progressing, and utilising what you have taught them.

The qualities discussed below as to what makes a good ESL teacher are relevant regardless of the subject you are teaching, and no matter what type of student is being educated.

Build a Genuine Connection with Students

Teachers who genuinely care about their students will have a profound influence on the students' behaviour, motivation and thinking. The students will respond to your sincerity; and in turn they will work harder, faster, and will learn more.

Think back to your own experiences at school, who would you respond better to in class: a teacher who you knew cared about you as a person? Or, the one who took everything far too seriously and was uninvolved with you personally?

Find the right balance, you don't want to be super serious; but at the same time you don't want to come across as a pushover either. Have fun where possible, but let the students know that you are serious too. Every school has their own set of rules and disciplinary actions for students - so find out what they are beforehand.

The relationship between a student and their teacher goes hand-in-hand with how well that student performs, and their success as a learner in the classroom. So always remember to give positive feedback, rather than negative; and no matter how small the accomplishment, always give them some praise. It's possible to correct students in a subtle manner; as opposed to disheartening them by over-emphasising that they are wrong or by broadcasting their mistakes.

Don't Forget to Smile

This might sound like an obvious one, but happiness really does breed happiness. Did you know that smiling is what's known as a mirror neuron? What this means is that when a human being sees somebody smile at them, the neurons respond and 'mirror' the action that they are observing from this person.

Of course walking around with a permanent grin on your face would be unnerving; however, a pleasant smile will give your students some added comfort, and create a more fun atmosphere within the classroom.

Be Creative in How You Communicate

People learn in different ways: verbally, visually or kinesthetically. There is more to communication than simply words. Make sure that when you are teaching that you are using different methods to convey the lesson.

It might seem a bit awkward initially; but accentuating your mouth as you speak words will benefit the students, and will allow you to speak slightly slower and more clearly. This will also help you to eradicate any strong regional accent you may have - as you will want to teach with a more neutral English accent.

Furthermore, give the lesson some variety by: writing on the board, or by getting the students to write on the board - so they get to see the written form in addition to the verbal form of the words. Be creative and/or animated with body language; use hand gestures, and signals to transmit your teachings. This will help the students to absorb the information; and more often than not, will never fail to make the students laugh as it keeps the lesson lighter.

Be Strategic

There will be times when students lose focus, or give you a blank look if they don't understand you - so be sure to persevere and try a different approach. If you ask your students "do you understand?" they will typically respond by saying yes; but more often than not that this means no. There are ways to test their comprehension by asking them to explain your instructions back to you, or you can rephrase what you said in the first place to ensure that they have understood.

It can also be sometimes frustrating for you when your students aren't producing the level of English that you know they are capable of. It's important to remember that whilst they have the vocabulary stored, they are still developing their skills of production. As a teacher, you must be patient and you must encourage them with this process, and realise that in the future they will be able to converse fluently.

Furthermore, games are an excellent way for the students to learn. You should use playing games to your advantage: the students think they're just having fun, but they are in fact learning as well. Playing hangman or "Pictionary" is always a good way to your lesson up and go over some of the vocabulary that the students have learned in class.

Some teachers will base their entire lessons around playing games. Obviously this depends on the age and level (perhaps excluding kindergarten); but it's not generally advised to spend the whole lesson playing clown.

Be Respectful to Every Student and Learn Names

One of the most essential components to being a teacher is learning your students' names. They are people, and deserve to be identified as such. If you don't bother learning their names then you're projecting a lack of respect, and you're going to make your job even harder down the line; especially when you need to call upon them to participate in class. Make a note of their names and their seating arrangements in a notebook; that way you will soon enough put a face to a name.

Some students will have tricky names to pronounce which often prompts teachers into assigning them an English name. The majority of students won't have an issue with this; however, giving a student an English name can be devaluing in some cultures. Try to avoid doing this, and instead ask the student what they would like to be called if you do encounter this problem. Also, learning how to read the language of the country you teach in will aid you massively when it comes to trying to pronounce the students' names.

Assess the Needs of Each Student

Learn to manage your time effectively and give focus to everyone's abilities in speaking, listening, reading and writing. If you track how your students are progressing as an individual, then you will know what types of lesson to teach to benefit them most. When you're new to the teaching game, it's possible to pay attention more to the loud outgoing students, so be mindful of that too.

Something that every teacher, new or old, is guilty of is unintentionally overlooking certain students, for example: the quiet ones. Sometimes there is just not enough time in a 40- or 50-minute lesson to pay attention to every tiny detail within the classroom, especially with voluminous classes.

Whilst there are a lot of different personalities in one room, it does not mean that you can't adapt your lesson to benefit every student. If a student is quiet by comparison, it does not mean that their level is lower - you will just need to find ways to give them more confidence and let them prosper. If a student is good at speaking, but you have noticed their sentence structuring, or grammar is poor, then designate a lesson to that.

Continuous assessment of your students will keep you one step ahead of what, and how something needs to be taught; and will ultimately help the students develop their English speaking skills quicker, and help them to build more self-confidence.

Always Encourage English Speaking Inside and Outside of the Classroom

Last, but by no means least - you should always encourage your students to speak English at any given opportunity. Some of the 'cheekier' students will use speaking in their native language against you - so you should be looking to nip this in the bud early on; and perhaps establish a set of house rules as to when they can and cannot speak in their first language in the classroom.

A lot of the teachers from the country you decide to teach will teach English lessons in their native language. This is favorable in some ways; but it doesn't give students the opportunity to immerse themselves in the language they are learning. It's therefore paramount for you to implement English speaking in your classrooms whenever and wherever you can such as: when they are doing a group activity, and/or when they are required to talk to each other. As mentioned previously, just because they don't understand every word you are saying literally, it doesn't mean there aren't other ways of communicating your message.

Bear in mind that whilst speaking English in the classroom is crucial, there are always going to be times when the students will have to revert back to their mother tongue - it's part and parcel of learning process. Also, there will be instances where the students can help each other to understand; allow this to happen as not only does the student with the question benefits, but so too does the student who is giving the explanation as they are validating the concept of the target language. If you can speak the local language, then by all means translate words or sentences if they're struggling to process what you have said in English.

In terms of outside the classroom, impart the advantages of them watching movies, or learning their favourite song lyrics in English. If they can learn the language by doing an extra-curricular activity that they are interested in, then that's an added bonus.

Enjoy the Experience

Overall, always keep an open mind and soak up the pleasures of teaching in a different culture. Kids have engaging minds; and in many countries it's usual for them to want to get to know their teacher on a more personal level, unlike conventions in the West. Whilst some of their questions ("are you married, teacher?"), or behaviour may seem intrusive or disrespectful to you at first, you will soon come to realise that it's not intentional - it's just a different approach to life, so embrace it. This is your time to shine. Good luck on your journey!

Bonus Chapter: Getting in to Teach English as a "Non-native" English speaker

I would like to acknowledge a strange and somewhat darker aspect of this perhaps over-glamorised global industry. Not all first language English speakers are recognised equally.

What makes a "Native English Speaker" a native English speaker?

That is that the term "Native" English speaker does not mean someone with full native proficiency in English. It doesn't mean someone for whom English is their mother tongue or their preferred language. It means anyone with US, UK, Ireland, South Africa, Canada, Australia or New Zealand citizenship. This is particularly bizarre since those for whom English is a first language may have been raised anywhere in the world.

Are non-native English speakers less qualified to teach than native English speakers?

Many citizens of the listed countries do not speak English as well and understand far less of its grammar and structure as they often have not been well instructed in English language themselves. Those for whom English is not their mother tongue but an acquired language may have a far stronger understanding of the rules of good English and be able to explain parts and figures of speech better than so-called "Native English" speakers. There is a lot of prejudice in hiring in this field. Let us acknowledge the beast and overcome it.

If English is your mother tongue, as it is for many from countries throughout the former Commonwealth and outside of it, you face a harder challenge in landing work teaching ESL.

Where could you teach?

First language English speakers from Africa can find work teaching in Central and South America. Cambodia and Thailand also accept ESL teachers with African citizenship. (South Africa is an exception as SA citizens qualify as "Native English" speakers.)

First language English speakers from Asia can successfully apply for work in Central and South America.

Citizens of Central or South America can teach ESL there or in Cambodia, Thailand and Turkey.

Teachers with citizenship in any of the Caribbean islands can find work in China or Japan but those countries have very strict hiring standards. For example, in Japan, citizens of non-native English speaking countries would need a four-year degree and 12 years of documented experience teaching at an all English school to be considered for employment.

EU citizens can find work in other parts of the EU, given that their English is excellent.

Turkey is an option for non-native speakers with at least a Bachelor's degree and a TEFL certification.

To get into Thailand, you would need a TOEIC (Test of English for International Communication) score of 600+ or IELTS (International English Language Testing System) score of 5+

and a four-year college degree in addition to a TEFL certification.

Cambodian standards are quite low, and the pay is correspondingly low too. As a non-native English speaker, a degree and a TEFL certification would give you a leg up.

South and Central American countries prefer TEFL certification in their country and generally they insist on TEFL certification. They are less concerned about whether you are a native or non-native speaker according to the ESL definition.

How Filipinos can do well teaching abroad

If you grew up in the Philippines, you would have grown up speaking English and Tagalog. The prejudice against hiring well qualified ESL teachers of Filipino origin, even with their excellent command of English is hard to justify but it is a reality. Nonetheless, there are ways of getting into this industry even with a Philippine citizenship.

Why Filipinos make excellent English language teachers

On the other hand, the Philippines was a US colony for 50 years and besides their naturally American English accent, thousands of Filipinos have been trained to sound American to serve call centres that require operators to sound like they are calling from mainland USA. This means that for students wanting to learn to speak like a native English speaker, the Philippines is a good place to go. The rates are a third or less of what a US or UK English language school would charge and for the same service standard. Naturally, the numbers of foreign students pouring into the Philippines to learn English has almost doubled every year for the past decade.

But as a Filipino wanting to teach ESL abroad, a TEFL certification is a prerequisite for getting started. Being a "non-native" English speaker means you would likely need a very high IELTS or TOEFL test score as well. Volunteering or getting paid experience back home is a very good idea but not always easy given the unemployment rate.

Network and put yourself out there

It is also essential to network. Put yourself out there on Facebook, freelancing profiles, ESL teaching platforms and meet people who are doing what you want to do. For Filipinos, the best places to teach ESL are Vietnam and Thailand - with low living costs and a high regard for Filipinos.

Get a firm grasp on the visa and work permit requirements. Some Asian and Middle Eastern countries have very strict checks and controls. In others, particularly in South America, schools almost encourage teachers to work illegally on a tourist visa.

Where Filipinos are succeeding in teaching English

Vietnam

It is best to get TEFL certification in the Philippines and then enter Vietnam and apply for work permits from there. Put together a detailed course log and highlight your experience. Apply for work by walking in to language institutes and introducing yourself. Get your work permit when you already have a job offer inside the country.

Thailand

The booming tourism industry in Thailand means that the need for English is higher than ever. Hundreds of Filipino ESL teachers are stepping over and earning this way.

Pick your destination and with a lot of guts and gumption, you can make it work.

Here are a few tips for going about that:

Don't hope for prejudice

It can be hard after facing numerous disappointments not to allow fatalism to creep in. But, if you expect the people you meet to be prejudiced against you, it will affect the way you present yourself. Don't introduce yourself as a non-native English speaker. If English is your first language, an employer will hear your voice and relax, confident that you are the right person for the job.

Be confident

Confidence and professional presentation go a long way. Fear, preempting disappointment and the suspicion of racial prejudice can show through and that can close doors even more than actual prejudice because it affects your view of yourself more even than their view of you, all other things being equal. You speak with the right accent, you understand the grammar and structure of English well and you are absolutely qualified to teach ESL to anyone who needs to learn it - project that confidence and you are well on your way.

ESL CLASSROOM GAMES
180 Educational Games and Activities for Teaching ESL/EFL Students
is now on promotion at <u>Amazon.com</u>

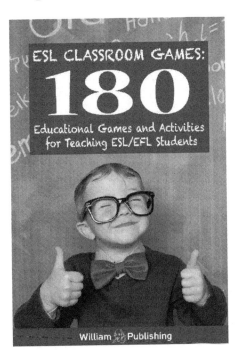

Save time on lesson planning, and make learning fun again. It includes a wide variety of reading, writing, speaking and listening games with emphasis on students' motivation, confidence, enjoyment and language retention.

Made in the USA
San Bernardino, CA
29 August 2017